Children and Bullying

Keeping Children Safe In Families and Communities

written by Terry Hitchcock
illustrated by Laurie Barrows

Text © 2018 Terry Hitchcock
Terryhitchcock@gmail.com
TerryHitchcock.com

Illustrations © 2018 Laurie Barrows
"Making the World a Happier Place,
One Smile at a Time" ™
LaurieBarrows@att.net
LaurieBarrows.com

ISBN 13: 978-1-7321520-2-1

Printed in the United States of America

Published in the United States of America

dedicated to our grandchildren,
Connor Peck
Ryan Peck

The subject of bullying is an issue for both our children as well as our adults, whatever age. This book is focused on our future, our children (The companion book focuses on *Adults and Bullying*).

83% of girls and 79% of boys report being bullied at school or on the internet

What is bullying?
Bullying is unwanted, aggressive behavior. Bullying can affect anyone. Kids who are bullied and who bully others may have serious, lasting problems over one's lifetime.

Types of bullying

Social bullying
This involves damaging a person's
reputation or relationships and includes:
Spreading rumors about someone
Leaving someone out on purpose

Telling other children not to be friends with someone
Embarrassing someone in public

Verbal bullying includes saying or writing mean things and includes:
Name-calling
Taunting
Teasing
Inappropriate sexual comments
Threatening to cause harm

Physical bullying involves hurting a person's body or possessions and includes:
Tripping and pushing
Making mean or rude hand gestures
Hitting, kicking and pinching
Spitting
Taking or breaking someone's things

When and where bullying happens: Bullying can occur during or after school hours. Most reported bullying happens in the school building and also on the playground or the bus. It can also happen travelling to or from school, at home, in the youth's neighborhood, or on the Internet.

Who is at risk?

Bullying can happen anywhere: cities; suburbs; or rural towns. Depending on the environment, some groups, such as lesbian, gay, bisexual, transgender or questioning (LGBTQ) youth, youth with disabilities, and socially isolated youth, may be at an increased risk of being bullied.

Effects of bullying

Bullying can affect everyone: those who are bullied; those who bully; and those who witness bullying. Bullying is linked to many negative outcomes including impacts on mental health, substance use, and suicide. It is important to talk to kids to determine whether bullying, or something else, is a concern.

Race, religion and diversity

Schools and communities that respect diversity can help protect children against bullying behavior. However, when children perceived as different are not in supportive environments, they may be at a higher risk of being bullied.

Disability and special needs

Children with disabilities; such as physical, developmental, intellectual, emotional, and sensory disabilities, are at an increased risk of being bullied. Any number of factors; physical vulnerability, social skill challenges, or intolerant environments, may increase the risk.

Kids with special health needs, such as epilepsy or food allergies, also may be at higher risk of being bullied. Bullying can include making fun of kids because of their allergies or exposing them to the things they are allergic to. In these cases, bullying is not just serious, it can mean life or death.

Cyber bullying

Cyber bullying is bullying that takes place over digital devices like cell phones, computers, and tablets. Cyber bullying includes sending, posting, or sharing negative, harmful, false, or mean content about someone else. It can include sharing personal or private information about someone else causing embarrassment or humiliation. Some cyber bullying crosses the line into unlawful or criminal behavior.

- 1 in 7 students in grades K – 12 are either a bully or have been a victim of bullying.
- An estimated 160,000 U.S. children miss school every day due to fear of attack or intimidation by other students.
- 35% of kids have been threatened online.
- Nearly 9 out of 10 LGBTQ youth report being verbally harassed at school in the past year because of their sexual orientation.
- 57% of boys and 43% of girls reported being bullied because of religious or cultural differences.
- Bullies often go on to perpetrate violence later in life: 40% of boys identified as bullies in grades 6 through 9 had three or more arrests by age 30.
- One out of every 10 students who drop out of school does so because of repeated incidents of bullying.
- 43% of kids have been bullied online, 1 in 4 have had it happen more than once.

How to prevent bullying

Parents, school staff, and other caring adults have a role to play in preventing bullying. They can:
• Talk about what bullying is and how to stand up to it safely. Tell kids bullying is unacceptable. Make sure kids know how to get help.
• Check in with kids often. Listen to them. Know their friends, ask about school, and understand their concerns.
• Encourage kids to do what they love. Special activities, interests, and hobbies can boost confidence, help kids make friends, and protect them from bullying behavior.
• Model with kindness and respect.

Notes, Ideas & Actions

Notes, Ideas & Actions

Notes, Ideas & Actions

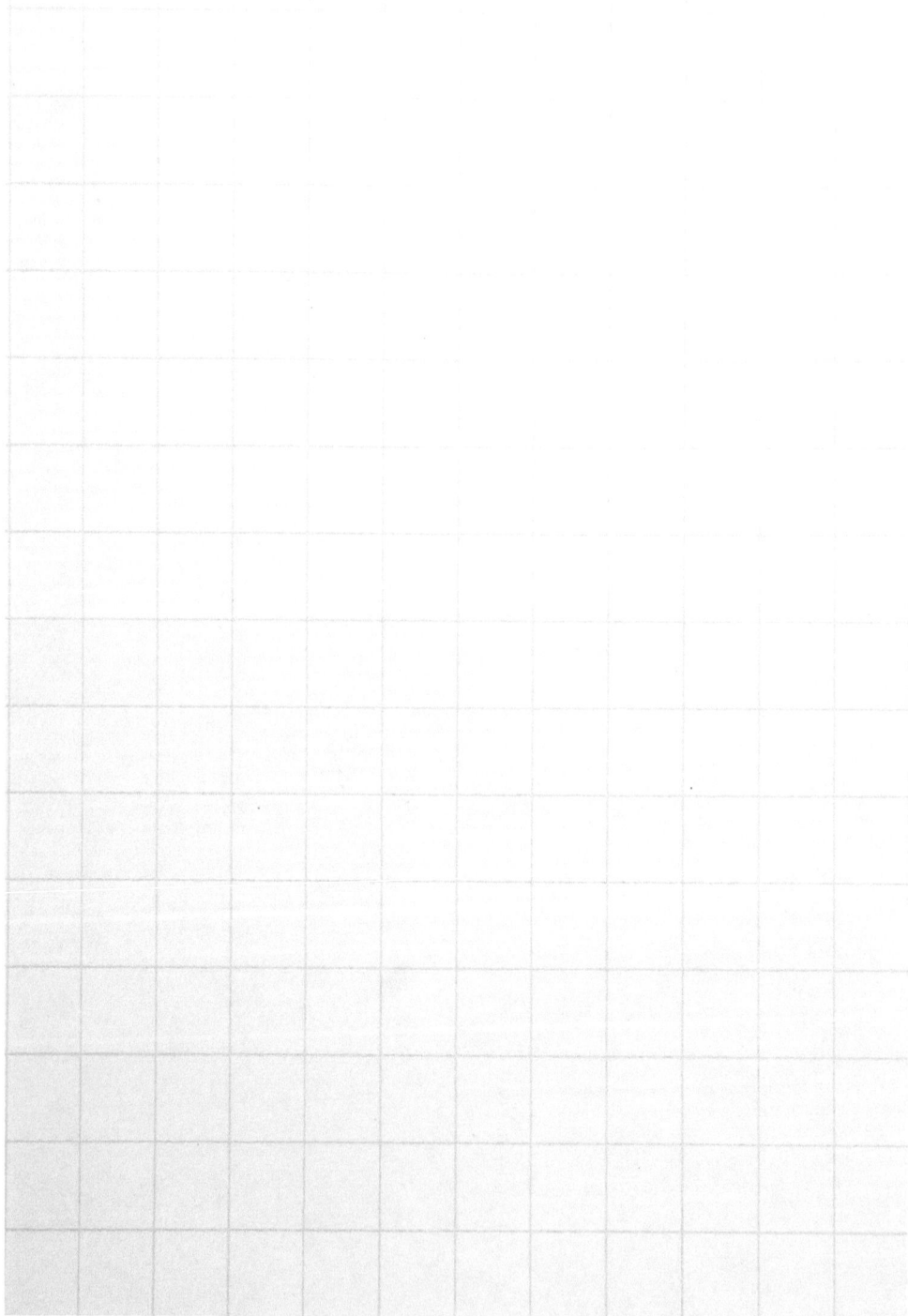

Notes, Ideas & Actions

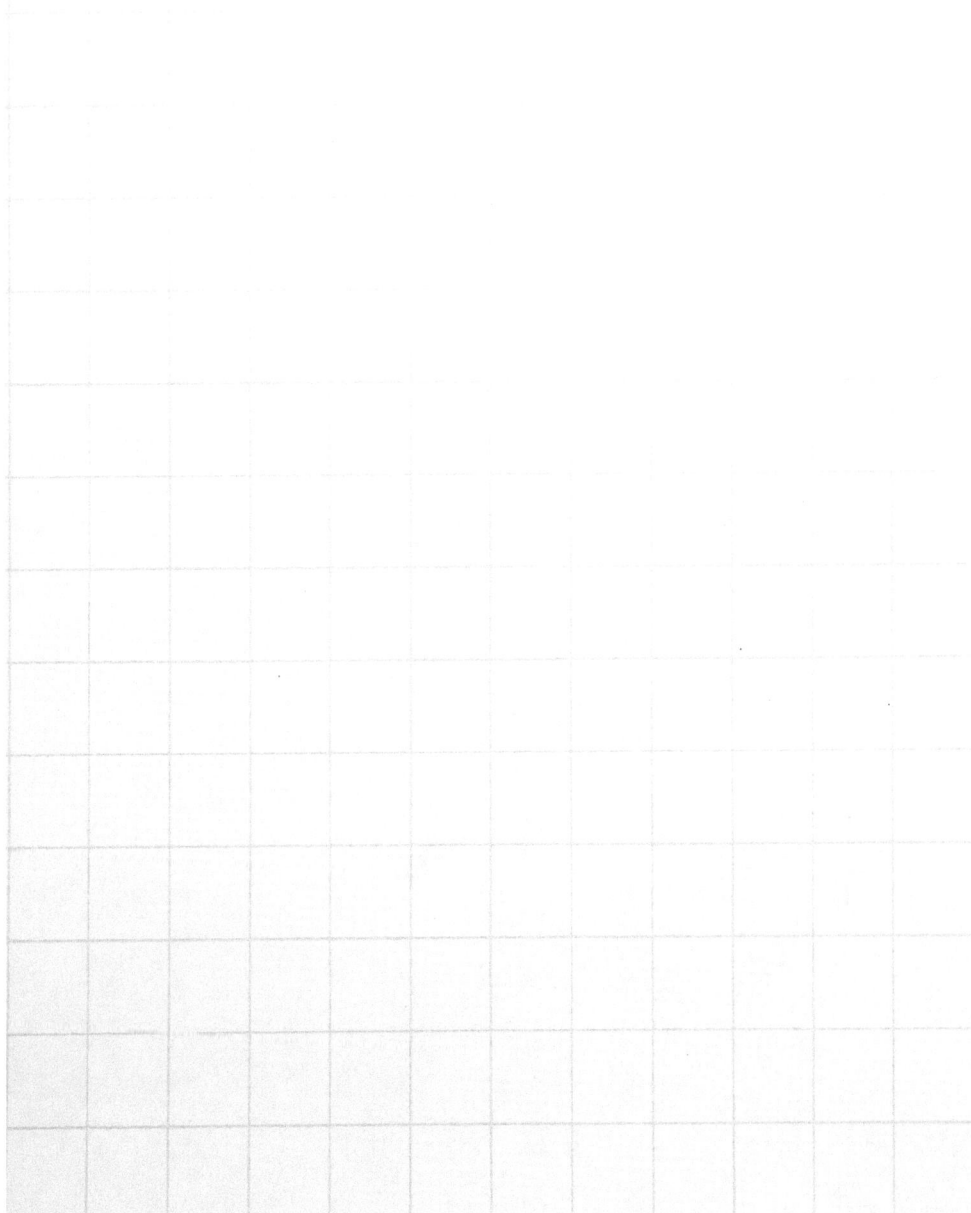

Notes, Ideas & Actions

Notes, Ideas & Actions

Notes, Ideas & Actions

Notes, Ideas & Actions

ABOUT THE AUTHOR

In 1996, Terry ran for children, the equivalent of a marathon or more each day for 75 consecutive days, arriving at the Opening Ceremonies of the Summer Olympics. He knew that his banner to carry for life was to honor our future, our children. From that point, Terry speaks all over the country to benefit our children.

This book, *Children and Bullying*, is an important topic that has destroyed or taken away precious lives each day in our communities. We don't talk about it and many don't recognize it happening. It is.

His first successful book, *American Business: The Last Hurrah?* tells the story of our country's successes and failures in 1984. One of his recent books, *A Father's Odyssey*, received the prestigious DOVE Award and now is read in over 27 countries. Hollywood produced a successful documentary of part of Terry's life called MY RUN and now a feature film, Pushing Life, is planned for production.

Terry and his wife Jean reside in Clearwater, Florida

TerryHitchcock.com
TerryHitchcock@gmail.com

ABOUT THE ILLUSTRATOR

MISSION STATEMENT:
"Making the World A Happier Place, One Smile at a Time."™

"Art should be fun!" states illustrator Laurie Barrows. The artist's work sparkles with playfulness. Her positive approach to life shines through. Bright color celebrates the joy the artist finds in her subject.
This is her 221st book

"I carry my philosophy of life into my work. I believe in a positive attitude and the power of love," says Barrows, "My goal with children's art is to touch lives with the wonderful luxury of innocence by creating positive images for the young."

"Children need a positive and empowering environment in which to grow and flourish. Children need freedom to dream. Everyday should be a celebration of joy and wonder. Developing a sense of self through play fosters creativity, imagination, and problem solving. We can all benefit by returning to a simpler time, if only for a moment."

"Success has many definitions. If my work makes you smile, and brightens your day, I've been successful."

LaurieBarrows.com
LaurieBarrows@att.net

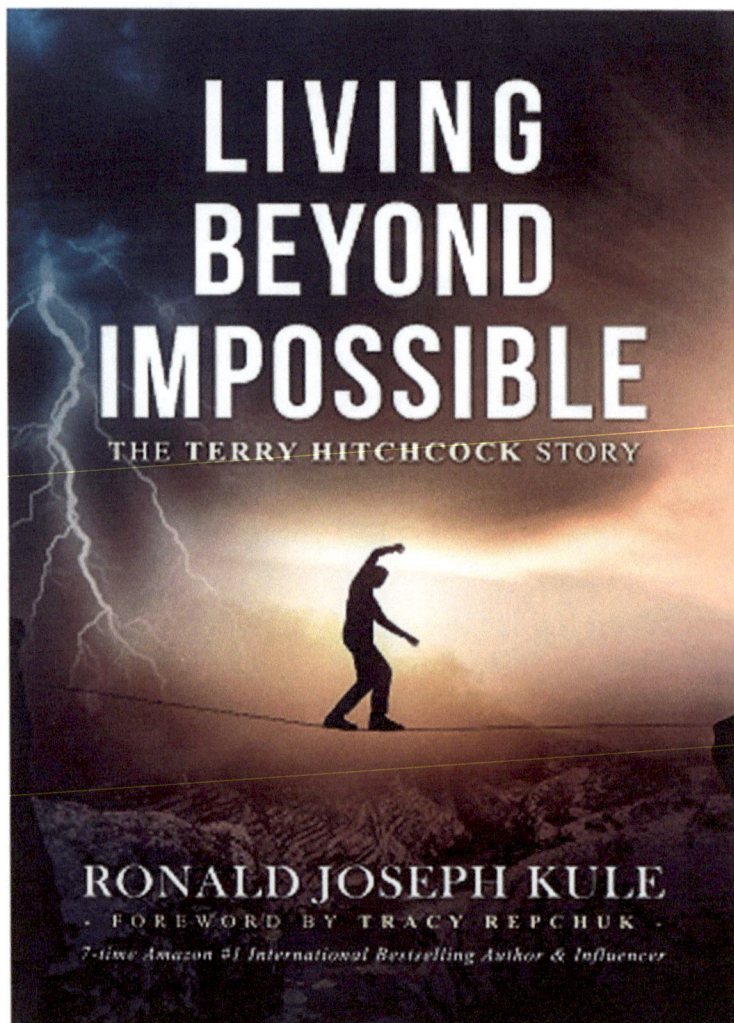

www.ingramcontent.com/pod-product-compliance
Lightning Source LLC
Chambersburg PA
CBHW041807040426
42448CB00005B/296